# THE FACE OF DIVINE DESTINY

*A Look at God's Divine Destiny in Blessings, in Tragedy of Deception, in Good and Evil, in Restoring a Nation, and in a Crazy Upside-Down World*

## JOHN MARINELLI

*The Face of Divine Destiny*
*A Look at God's Divine Destiny In Blessings, In Tragedy of Deception, In Good and Evil, In Restoring a Nation, And In a Crazy Upside-Down World*
Copyright © 2023 John Marinelli
Ocala, Florida …All rights reserved.

First Edition: 8/2023

Print ISBN: 978-1-0882-3270-5
eBook ISBN: 978-1-0882-3273-6

Cover and Formatting: Streetlight Graphics
Contact: johnmarinelli@embarqmail.com

This book is protected under US copyright laws. Any reproduction or other use is prohibited without the written permission of the author.

No part of this book may be reproduced, scanned, or distributed in any printed or electronic form without permission. Please do not participate in or encourage piracy of copyrighted materials in violation of the author's rights. Thank you for respecting the hard work of this author.

# TABLE OF CONTENTS

Preface ............................................................................. 1

Introduction ..................................................................... 3

Chapter One ..................................................................... 5

Chapter Two: ................................................................... 17

Chapter Three ................................................................. 29

Chapter Four ................................................................... 39

Rest My Child ................................................................. 43

Chapter Five .................................................................... 47

Conclusion ...................................................................... 53

About The Author John Marinelli ................................. 54

Gallery of Encouraging Christian Poems ....................... 55

# PREFACE

The purpose of this book is to showcase the sovereignty of God in the Old Testament as seen through the eyes of Romans 8:28-30. Seeing this promise operating in the lives of Old Testament saints is a real eye opener, especially when the principles of that promise can be clearly seen and applied to New Testament times and the lives of modern-day saints.

My goal is to explain the truths and discuss the possibilities as well as the real and alternate realities that were realized by God's chosen people. I will show God's divine destiny in contrast to alternate destinies that played out in the lives of the Old and New Testament saints. I will also show how current day saints are affected.

My reason for authoring this book is because God's children need to know how God works in the lives of his saints and the world at large. This is an easy read with lots of Bible support.

# INTRODUCTION

"The Face of Divine Destiny" is a study of God's divine destiny in the lives of Old and New Testament saints. It is an attempt, by the author, to capture the ebb and flow of life's path towards eternity. We will use the Biblical character, Abraham, from the Old Testament and his family to track the movement of God's "Divine Will" among his children.

We will also examine the face of divine destiny through the eyes of Romans 8:28-30 found in the New Testament. We will see it in blessings, in tragedy, In the power of good and evil, in restoration and in today's crazy upside-down world.

We will also address the theological implications of the "Sovereignty of God" and the "Free Will" of man as they interact in real life situations.

Current day lifestyle applications will also be discussed that apply to Christian doctrine in modern-day times.

# CHAPTER ONE

## The Face of Divine Destiny In The Blessings of God

Our story and Bible study begins with God's divine destiny centered in the life of Abraham. Here is the scriptural account, commonly known as "The Abrahamic Covenant."

"The LORD had said to Abram, 'Leave your country, your people and your father's household and go to the land I will show you. I will make you into a great nation and I will bless you; I will make your name great, and you will be a blessing. I will bless those who bless you, and whoever curses you I will curse; and all peoples on earth will be blessed through you" (Genesis 12:1-3).

Notice the blessings that come with God's divine destiny.

1.  *"I will make you into a great nation"*

This is the blessing of authority, power and dominion. Abraham was promoted to being the head and not the tail. He was given the favor of God and the counsel of divine wisdom to execute the will of God in his life.

Can you imagine Abraham telling those around him, "I am going to bring forth a great nation upon the earth." I can see the people of his day telling him, "Who Said So?" and Abraham saying, "God Said So." Then the people laughing, and replying, "Right!"

Sometimes when God tells you what's going to happen in your future, it is a big pill to swallow. Most will not agree with you and others even laugh in your face because it doesn't seem possible to them. Nevertheless, if God says it, we are to say, "Yes Lord" and believe it with all of our hearts.

Abraham believed God, and it was accounted unto him for righteousness. Genesis 15:6 He was seen as a righteous man because he believed what God said would indeed come to pass. When we believe, we rely upon, adhere to, and trust in what God has spoken into our lives.

We do not believe and adhere to our own lustful wants. I can say that I am believing for a new house or Cadillac but if God didn't speak it into my ear, chances are it will never happen. It has to be in accordance to what God said, not friends, neighbors or anyone other than God.

It's all about listening to the voice of God and trusting in him to accomplish what he says. Here's how the Bible says it, "So shall my word be that goes forth out of my mouth: it shall not return unto me void, but it shall accomplish that which I please, and it shall prosper *in the thing* whereto I sent it." Isaiah 55:11

Abraham could have said, "No Way, it just isn't happening. I am too old, too tired and too frightened" But he pushed all the negative voices outside of his hearing and focused on the future with a new excitement.

2. *"I will bless you;"*

What does it mean to be blessed by God? It's great to realize that you live under the blessing of God and not rejection. Blessings come in many ways. They can be material, Physical and spiritual, which were evident in Abraham's life.

The blessing of Abraham was a benefit to Abraham himself. In terms of the ancient world, he was a success: he was well-respected, he was healthy, and he had many descendants. This is just the beginning of blessings that helped to raise up Abraham in the eyes of those around him. There would be more to come.

3. *"I will make your name great."*

Now God just promised to make the name of Abraham great; That means a man of stature; A man of good reputation; A man known for his integrity; Honest, trust-worthy and so on.

Being great comes with the attraction of many friends and possibly even more enemies. It's a lot to live up to and you need to be very focused upon God's will so you don't get egotistic and fall away from that honored seat. You also have to ignore the critics that badmouth you for being and doing good. Abraham must have known this and did it all the time.

4. "You will be a blessing"

If God gives you more than you can use in material passions, he is setting you up to be a blessing to others. We do not want to hold material blessings so tight that others cannot benefit from our overflow. I can remember a time that a man had his bike stolen. It was the only transportation he had. No one in the church helped him to replace his bike.

I prayed about helping him and asked the Lord to bless me so I could be a blessing to him. the very next day, I won a sales contest at work that put $100 cash in my hand. I thanked the Lord and gave the money to the guy so he could replace his bike. I was glad that I could be a blessing. When was the last time you asked God to bless you so you could be a blessing to someone else?

I am sure that Abraham also had many divine appointments to be a blessing to others. You know how I know? Because God said he would make Abraham a blessing to others. He'd have to give him the where-with-all to do so.

5. "I will bless those who bless you"

Imagine that! God will bless everyone that blesses Abraham. Remember, there is no nation, no 12-tribes, only one man, standing alone before God. I think the difference between Abraham and today's Christian believer is Abraham stood in an unbelievable faith. He actually believed that all of this 7-point blessing would happen and he acted upon it in his daily life.

I can see how that might play out in Abraham's mindset. He probably rejoiced at the idea of being blessed by others and saw that blessing coming to him by the hand of God. It is truly great to see the hand of God in your life helping you to grow, prosper and dwell in peace.

***News Flash!!!*** The Bible tells us that, well, let me quote the scripture so there is no confusion.

"So then they which be of faith are blessed with faithful Abraham." Colossians 3:9

Let's look at it from the Berean Standard Version…"The Scripture foresaw that God would justify the Gentiles by faith, and foretold the gospel to Abraham"

*"All nations will be blessed through you." So those who have faith are blessed along with Abraham, the man of faith. All who rely on works of the law are under a curse. For it is written: "Cursed is everyone who does not continue to do everything written in the Book of the Law." Colossians 3:8-10*

We are privileged to participate in the blessings of God upon Abraham simply by believing the gospel and trusting in God to bring about his divine destiny in our lives.

If we walk by faith, we will see the hand of God in our lives and will experience prosperity by divine decree. Remember, our walk of faith connects with Abraham's walk of faith, qualifying us to be blessed with him.

I heard a story by a preacher a while back. It was an illustration in his sermon so I am not sure if it is a true story but it makes the point. The story goes like this:

An old lady who lived alone, back in the eighteen hundreds, needed to chop wood for her cooking and heating. She obviously couldn't do it because of her old age. So, as was her custom, she would stand on her front porch and pray in a loud voice to God for help.

The 1st day, during her prayer for help, a man passed by and laughed at her saying, "How silly, does she think that God will show up and chop her wood?" He passed on by shaking his head at the old lady's prayer.

This continued for 3-4 days as the man passed by every day. On the 5th day, the man picked up the axe and chopped the old lady's wood, complaining all the time. The old lady began to praise God for the wood being chopped.

The moral of the story is that there will be times in your life when God might bring a "Wood Chopper" to assist you. Your prayer gets answered but in a most unusual way. So, if you walk in faith like Abraham did, you will be blessed along with him in a whole bunch of different ways.

6. "and whoever curses you I will curse"

This is a blessing of protection. The New Testament teaches this truth as well. Paul tells us that, "Be not deceived; God is not mocked: for whatsoever a man soweth, that shall he also reap" Galatians 6:7

In both cases, whether a direct curse from God or a seed of malice planted against you by an individual, God has your back. He will avenge you.

7. "and all peoples on earth will be blessed through you"

This is a prelude to the gospel message of the New Testament. It is a prophecy that foretells, in a shadow, the coming of a Messiah (Hebrew for the "Anointed One"). It would be a direct reference to Jesus, the Christ (Greek for, "The Anointed One") that came in the fullness of time to save us from our sin and bless us with his love and grace. He is the Savior of the world and the only way to God's blessings. See John 14:6

Let's look at a few more scriptures that discuss God's blessings:

- **Philippians 4:19** – "But my God shall supply all your need according to his riches in glory by Christ Jesus."

All your needs are not all your wants. Needs are usually aligned with God's will. Be sure you are sensitive to God's will because that is where your blessings and divine destiny are.

- **James 1:17** – "Every good gift and every perfect gift is from above, and cometh down from the Father of lights, with whom is no variableness."

A good and perfect gift is a blessing that has no hidden agenda. There is no torment or strings attached. God's gift fits perfect into our lives and brings peace to our souls. However, sometimes that which is to bless us shows up as a trial, testing our faith. The end of that thing is a blessing. That's happened to me several times.

- **Proverbs 10:22** - "The blessing of the LORD, it makes rich, and he adds no sorrow with it."

Blessings without sorrow, what a concept. Blessings that make us rich are those that flood our souls with peace, happiness and joy. It's not all about money.

- **Numbers 6:24-26** – "The LORD bless thee, and keep thee: The LORD make his face shine upon thee, and be gracious unto thee: The LORD lift up his countenance upon thee, and give thee peace."

We are indeed blessed when the Lord makes his face to shine upon us. The Jewish rabis called this the "Shekinah" glory. (a form of a Hebrew word that literally means "he caused to dwell," signifying that it was a divine visitation of the presence or dwelling of the Lord God on this earth.)

- **Isaiah 41:10** – "Fear thou not; for I am with thee: be not dismayed; for I am thy God: I will strengthen thee; yea, I will help thee; yea, I will uphold thee with the right hand of my righteousness."

When God says he is with us, he is. We do not have to be afraid anymore. I guess the correct slang for our generation is, "God's got your back"

- **3 John 1:2** – "Beloved, I wish above all things that thou may prosper and be in health, even as thy soul prospers."

The apostle John had a wish. It was that the believers of his day would prosper and be in good health. I think his wish still applies to our day. What do you think?

- **2 Corinthians 9:8** – "And God is able to make all grace abound toward you; that ye, always having all sufficiency in all things, may abound to every good work."

God's blessings are first of all by Grace (Unmerited Favor) that we might have all our needs met and then some, in order that we can participate in good works.

- **Proverbs 16:7** – "When a man's ways please the LORD, he makes even his enemies to be at peace with him."

The greatest blessing, in my opinion, is to live such a life that it pleases the Lord. It also keeps your enemies at a distance. That's a really good blessing in itself.

- **John 1:16** – "And of his fulness have all we received, and grace for grace."

The apostle John tells us that all of us have already received the fullness of God. Check our Galatians 5:22 to see what the fullness of God consists of.

- **Matthew 6:30-33** – "Wherefore, if God so clothe the grass of the field, which today is, and tomorrow is cast into the oven, shall he not much more clothe you, O ye of little faith?"

The children of little faith worry about tomorrow. However, see here where God is saying that he will take care of us. I believe it, do you?

- **Philippians 2:13** – "For it is God which worketh in you both to will and to do of his good pleasure."

We do not have to strive to try to figure out God's will and what he desires of us. If we are open to listen, he will work his desires into us so we feel them and want to act upon them as part of our fee will choices. Then he will give us the tools to accomplish all that suits his pleasure.

Blessings can come in many forms. According to the King James Version (KJV) of the Bible, here are three categories:

1. **Heavenly blessings:** blessings that come from God and are spiritual in nature, such as grace, peace, joy, etc.
2. **Earthly blessings:** blessings that come from the natural world and are material in nature, such as wealth, success, fame, etc.

3. **Physical/biological blessings**: blessings that come from the human body and are related to health, beauty, strength, etc.

Here is the blessing of God that came to us through Jesus as he fulfilled the promises God made to Abraham. Check it out:

"Blessed be the God and Father of our Lord Jesus Christ, who hath blessed us with all *spiritual blessings in heavenly places in Christ according as he hath chosen us in him before the foundation of the world*, that we should be holy and without blame before him in love, having *predestinated us unto the adoption of children by Jesus Christ to himself,* according to the good pleasure of his will, to the praise of the glory of his grace, wherein *he hath made us accepted in the beloved.* In whom we have redemption through his blood, the forgiveness of sins, according to the riches of his grace;

Wherein *he hath abounded toward us in all wisdom and prudence having made known unto us the mystery of his will,* according to his good pleasure which he hath purposed in himself that in the dispensation of the fulness of times *he might gather together in one all things in Christ, both which are in heaven, and which are on earth; even in him:*

In whom also *we have obtained an inheritance, being predestinated according to the purpose of him who worketh all things after the counsel of his own will:* That we should be to the praise of his glory, who first trusted in Christ. In whom ye also trusted, after that ye heard the word of truth, the gospel of your salvation: in whom also *after that ye believed, ye were sealed with that holy Spirit of promise,*

*Which is the earnest of our inheritance until the redemption of the purchased possession, unto the praise of his glory.* Wherefore I also, after I heard of your faith in the Lord Jesus, and love unto all the saints, cease not to give thanks for you, making mention of you in my prayers;

*That the God of our Lord Jesus Christ, the Father of glory, may give unto you the spirit of wisdom and revelation in the knowledge of him… The eyes of your understanding being enlightened; that ye may know what is the hope of his calling, and what the riches of the glory of his inheritance in the saints and what is the exceeding greatness of his power to us-ward who believe, according to the working of his mighty power, which he wrought in Christ, when he raised him from the dead, and set him at his own right hand in the heavenly places, far above all principality, and power, and might, and dominion, and every name that is named, not only in this world, but also in that which is to come and hath put all things under his feet, and gave him to be the head over all things to the church, which is his body, the fulness of him that fills all in all."* Ephesians 1:3-23

I realize this is quite a long scripture passage but I felt it necessary to show you how we fit into God's divine destiny.

Gotquestions.com tells us all about the Spiritual blessing we have in Christ. Take a read:

## What Are Spiritual Blessings?

Ephesians 1:3 says that we have been blessed with all spiritual blessings in Christ. What are these spiritual blessings, and what do they do for us? Contrary to some beliefs, they are not some mysterious power or cosmic connection reserved for a select few. They are the key benefits of a relationship with God through Jesus Christ.

The word blessing in Ephesians 1:3 is a translation of the Greek word eulogy and it means *"to speak well of."* Since God is the one acting in this verse, we can say that God has spoken good things about us, or pronounced good things for our benefit. The good things that God has decreed for us are probably beyond our ability to number, but we can outline a few by looking at the verses that follow the statement (Ephesians 1:4–13).

*The first blessing* listed is the election as saints. Ephesians 1:4 says that he has "chosen us in him before the foundation of the world, that we should be holy and without blame before him in love." God has chosen to make us holy and blameless, and all because of his love, his good pleasure, and his grace (verses 5–6). What a blessing, that "even when we were dead in sins" (Ephesians 2:5), God chose to extend his grace to us and offer us salvation. This is even more amazing when we realize that he made that decision before sin even entered into the world.

*The second blessing* listed is found in verse 5—our adoption as his children.

Not only has God chosen us to be made holy, but he grants us full status as his children, with all the benefits thereof. John 1:12 says, "As many as received him, to them gave he power to become the sons of God, even to them that believe on his name." When we believe the gospel, we receive full access to the Father, able to call out to him as his children.

*The third spiritual blessing* is in Ephesians 1:6, where we are *"accepted in the beloved."* The word is related to grace and gives the idea of making us graceful or favorable through Christ, the beloved of God. When we put on Christ, the Father sees his loveliness when he looks at us. The blood of Christ has taken away the guilt of our sins, and we stand before the Father as perfectly accepted.

This leads us right into *the fourth blessing* (Ephesians 1:7), the redemption through his blood. Redemption speaks of buying one's freedom, paying a ransom. The price for our sins, the payment to buy us out of eternal condemnation, was fully paid by the blood of Christ. In Christ, we are no longer slaves to sin, but we become slaves to God. Since we are bought and paid for by his blood, we have an obligation to glorify God in our body and spirit (1 Corinthians 6:20).

Ephesians 1:7 also describes *the fifth blessing*, the forgiveness of sins. It is closely related to redemption, but looks at the other side of the coin. In paying the ransom for our sins, the debt of sin was canceled, and we were forgiven. We no longer have the burden of guilt for violating God's holy laws.

The *sixth spiritual blessing* listed is knowing the mystery of his will (Ephesians 1:8–10). God has given us wisdom and insight through his Word and has shown us his desire to bring all things together to glorify Christ. Since all of creation was made by him and is for his good pleasure (Revelation 4:11), the consummation of his plan is when everything and everyone is brought in line to glorify him. By aligning ourselves with him by faith, we become part of his perfect plan and purpose.

Verse 11 says *another blessing* is available, the inheritance that is given to us through Christ. What is included in that inheritance? "But as it is written, Eye hath not seen, nor ear heard, neither have entered into the heart of man, the things which God hath prepared for them that love him" (1 Corinthians 2:9). The riches of glory, the presence of God, the eternal home – these don't even scratch the surface of all the blessings that belong to our inheritance.

*Yet another blessing* is found in Ephesians 1:13, which is the sealing of the Holy Spirit. When we become God's children, he places his mark of ownership on us, guaranteeing our eternal security. This is spoken of as the downpayment of our full redemption, to hold us until the day Christ brings us to him.

The list could go on and on speaking of the privileges that are ours in Christ. We are laborers together with God (1 Corinthians 3:9); we are ambassadors bringing the message of reconciliation to a foreign land (2 Corinthians 5:20); and we are the bride of Christ (2 Corinthians 11:2). We have available to us the peace that passes understanding (Philippians 4:7) and the assurance that nothing is able to separate us from the love of God that is in Christ Jesus (Romans 8:39).

## *How Do We Access All of These Blessings?*

They are readily accessible to everyone who is in Christ Jesus. The way to be in Christ is to repent, or turn away from our sins (Acts 17:30), confessing to God that we are sinners (Proverbs 28:13; Romans 10:9). When we believe that Christ died to take our punishment and now lives to give us new life (1 Corinthians 15:3–4), he grants us forgiveness of sins and all the blessings that accompany that salvation.

**Note:** Check out "The Divine Perspective", my new book was just published in August of 2023. You can see it and buy it at www.marinellichrikstianbooks.com

Abraham was aware of God's blessings. He could see them in his life and everyday experiences. He had a relationship with God and held him in high esteem. I wonder how many Christians do the same. Most of the folks I see that claim to be believers in God, have no practical relationship with him. They live in a superficial world of carnality with no real faith. They struggle with life and purpose for just being alive.

The biggest blessing of all seems to be a secret to modern day Christians. Here's what Paul said to the Galatians, "So then *they which be of faith* are blessed with faithful Abraham." Galatians 3:9

Do you get it? The faithful qualify for and participate in the blessings of Abraham, the father of faith. What exactly does that mean? I do not think it means that God is going to birth a great nation out of your loins, like he did with Abraham. However, the intent is to be blessed by God, which means you are under his protection and care. He sees you as his own and has granted you unmerited favor. This is New Testament grace.

I think Romans 8:28-30 expresses the heart of being blessed. I quoted this passage of scripture earlier in the book. The sum of it all is this:

God works everything out for good in the lives of those that fear (Reverence & Respect) him. His blessing is only for those that are called according to his purposes, which is divine destiny at work in the lives of those who walk by faith. Their destination (Destiny) has been predetermined (Predestinated) by God to be conformed to the image of his son. Why? so Jesus can be the 1st born of many brethren.

**Can you see the picture?** God called Abraham because he was open to his instruction and will. God is calling us because we are also open to his instruction and will. Our destiny, like Abraham's, is set by God to be like Jesus. Abraham was a type and shadow of what was to come. We are the real deal. It is actually happening in our lives.

We will look at this idea, "Working Out Everything For Good" as we continue our study. I think you will find it really interesting how God operates.

# CHAPTER TWO:

## The Face of Divine Destiny In The Tragedy of Deception

We have seen the blessings and favor given to Abraham by God. So, he prospered and had Isaac and Isaac had Jacob and Jacob had twelve sons and then came tragedy to his house. (I know I am leaving a lot of history out associated with Isaac & Jacob but I will discuss key points as I continue.)

The tragedy of deception really began with Jacob. Isaac had two sons, Esau and Jacob. Jacob bought the birthright from his brother for a pot of bean stew and deceived Isaac in his old age. By rights, the birthright should have been passed down to Esau.

It appears that Jacob did not actually inherit any property from his father, even though he did buy the birthright from Esau. What Jacob did receive from Isaac was the divine blessing planned for the first born male.

Apparently, the birthright didn't hold much value to Esau but was prized by Jacob. It was so valuable that he manipulated his brother and deceived his father to get it. This one action changed the face of divine destiny. Had it not happened, we would see the scriptures saying that God was the God of Abraham, Isaac and Esau, not Jacob.

However, God honored Jacob because he valued the birthright. So, what is it about the birthright that makes it so valuable?

Because Esau was born first, he would have normally received the birthright and blessing from his father, Isaac. (The birthright would give the son a bigger part of what the family owned and more authority. Since God had made big promises to Isaac, this birthright was a big deal.) But God had told Rebekah that their younger son, Jacob, would be blessed.

Jacob didn't have to resort to trickery and deceit but he did and it caused him to flee from his father's house and his brother's face. Esau ended up with the land but Jacob became one of the patriarchs that God used to identify himself. He also continued the lineage through which Jesus, the Anointed One, would come. That was the real value of the birthright and why Jacob wanted it.

I would think that Jacob knew that God had chosen him instead of Esau from an early age. His mother must have told him somewhere down the line before he lied to his father. Sometimes we can try to help God work out his plan and mess it up. Jacob and Esau didn't talk or see each other for many years. Isaac passed on with Jacob not being at his side. Esau and Jacob didn't reconcile until their old age.

So, Jacob moves on with his life and has twelve sons who form the 12-tribes of Israel, the nation that God promised Abraham. It is here, in the lives of the 12 sons that Romans 8:28 plays a big role.

If you remember the story, Jacob had a son late in his life. He named him Joseph. The boy was his favorite. He even made a multicolor coat for him and spoiled him on many occasions…so much so, that Joseph boasted to his older brothers, sharing his dreams that they would be his servants one day.

To make a long story short, the anger of his older brothers kindled until they couldn't take it anymore. They rose up together, dug a pit and tossed Joseph into it. They were going to leave him there to die. But a caravan heading to Egypt passed by and they sold Joseph to them. His fate would now be determined in the Egyptian slave market.

This turn of events would again change the face of divine destiny. Had it not happened, the entire family would have stayed where they were and prospered as God originally wanted. However, as it played out, Joseph was sold in Egypt, went to prison on a trumped-up charge for several years. Then he interpreted the Pharoah's dream and moved from the prison to the palace to become Pharoah's right-hand man. He brought his entire family to Egypt, abandoning the promised land, which was God's divine destiny for them.

That one decision to sell Joseph led all of them to be blessed. I guess they all thought that the grass on another side of the street was greener…But it never last unless it is from God. Another Pharoah came to power that didn't know Joseph and they all went into slavery for over 400 years.

It didn't have to happen, but it did, because of the choices of the brothers and the boasting of being superior from Joseph. It is a prime example of man's free will and God's sovereignty. It is also a perfect example of Romans 8:28 as God now has to shift gears and work everything together for good.

Joseph's tragic ordeal changed the face of divine destiny. The promise to Abraham had successfully been defeated and the divine plan of God stopped dead in its tracks. However, the story didn't end there. It never ends with man's choices because God is greater and he is sovereign, which means, he can override our choices and/or work around them to accomplish his own will.

Here's how I see Sovereignty and "Free Will." They operate together but to see the process in action, sometimes, you need to look down through the centuries.

Let's consider God, for the moment, as an Architect. He created everything; the stars, the planets, the animals, and yes, even man, no matter who says otherwise.

When it came to creating man, he had to know the beginning of each life and its end. He had to know every interaction and choice that every person would make. I can see all of this activity as the formation of a master plan that was made before it was activated, just like an Architect does before building a building.

Once the master plan is finished, construction begins as indicated in the 1$^{st}$ chapter of Genesis. God said, "Let there be" and it was. It happened according to his master plan. Even Jesus' birth, death, earthly ministry and becoming the sacrificial Lamb of God to pay for the sins of the entire world was known and planned before the foundation of the world. Hebrews 9:26 Time and eternity were both present at creation. This can also be seen in Matthew 6:31-34. Take a read:

*"Wherefore, if God so clothe the grass of the field, which today is, and tomorrow is cast into the oven, shall he not much more clothe you, O ye of little faith? Therefore take no thought, saying, What shall we eat? or, What shall we drink? or, Wherewithal shall we be clothed? (For after all these things do the Gentiles seek:) for your heavenly Father knows that ye have need of all these things.*

*But seek ye first the kingdom of God, and his righteousness; and all these things shall be added unto you. Take therefore no thought for the morrow: for the morrow shall take thought for the things of itself. Sufficient unto the day is the evil thereof."*

Before anything was created, God made a master plan that included your life and your needs. His provision is waiting for the time of your need to arrive. God sees what your choices will be and works around them if necessary to accomplish his will. He is not interested in how long that will take. He is interested in meeting your needs as they arise. This way of doing things allows God's Sovereignty to remain in full force as you exercise your "Free Will" choices. That's why it is so important to seek the Lord for direction, so the timelapse between what God has to do and what you are doing will be shortened.

In the case of Joseph and the 400 years of bondage, the choices made actually extended the time it took for God to work everything together for their good. Think about it. I'll say it again…Had not Joseph's brothers sold him into slavery and had not Joseph made them angry about being their ruler someday, they would have stayed in the promised land and continued to be blessed and prosper into the nation God promised Abraham.

I know what you might be thinking…what about the famine and the need to go to Egypt to buy grain? Some theologians see Joseph's ordeal as God's divine will to save Abraham's family. However, putting all of them in a state of slavery for over 400 years under a tyrannical Pharoah and an ungodly nation is far from God's provision.

Nevertheless, God knowing that the brother's choices would send the family to Egypt, he used the circumstance to provide through Joseph, even though they were to live out an alternate reality, not originally selected by him. This is how Romans 8:28 applies to the story and how the same logic comes into play in our lives.

We make mistakes, bad choices and even a little rebellion now and them but God is true to his word and will accomplish it, no matter how long it takes. Sometimes we think we have gotten away with doing our own will opposed to the will of God. That is just not true. He knows the beginning from the end and, like the elephant, never forgets.

I have known times when I forgot all about a certain thing but years later discover it in my life and remember that it was a prayer prayed over many years ago.

One such instance was when I was in high school, I had a deep crush on a cheerleader. I went to all the games and watched her do her thing. She never knew my feelings but I sure did. We never got together.

Several years later I married, had two kids and ended up divorced after 10-years. In that time of rejection, self-doubt and pain, I prayed and asked the Lord for someone that could help me to get back into his divine will.

Then I went on in my misery until one day I meet the gal, fell in love and remarried, only to discover that she was just like what I imagined my high school cheerleader was like. Guess what? That's right, she was my cheerleader in full force. It's been over 40 years of continual blessings as my cheerleader wife stands by my side. God didn't forget.

So it was with the fledging nation of Israel before they became a nation. God didn't forget. In the fullness of time, he brought forth his will. God is always true to his word.

As you can probably see, God seems to be working around the will of man. He grants man the privilege to make his or her own choices, even though it might delay his divine will. It certainly gives us the opportunity to live out our own lives, do our own thing and shape our own destiny. That means we can decide what our future will look like before we enter it and make choices as to how to accomplish the end results.

The problem with all of this freedom is, we are not really knowledgably or mentally fit to make all the right decisions. Plus, we face opposition from outside sources, events and other pressures that do not want us to succeed.

The Jewish people were call, "Stiff Necks" by God. Gotdquesttions.com offers this explanation:

To be stiff-necked is to be obstinate and difficult to lead. The Bible often uses this figure of speech when describing the attitude of Israel toward God (e.g., Exodus 33:3; Deuteronomy 9:13; Nehemiah 9:16; Acts 7:51).

The term was originally used to describe an ox that refused to be directed by the farmer's ox goad. When a farmer harnessed a team of oxen to a plow, he directed them by poking them lightly with a sharp spike on the heels or the neck to make them pick up speed or turn.

An ox that refused to be directed in such a way by the farmer was referred to as "stiff-necked." A stiff-necked animal (or person) refuses to turn the head in order to take a different path.

The Israelites were familiar with the term *stiff-necked*, so when the Lord used it to describe them, they got the message. Every farmer understood the frustration of trying to plow a field or transport a cart when an ox was being stiff-necked. An ox that refused to be guided was useless for any real work. A stiff-necked ox was a disappointment in that it was not performing the task it was intended to perform.

God's chosen people refused to love him, honor him, and obey him, they were not living the purpose for which God chose them as his own (see Isaiah 41:8–9; Jeremiah 7:23–24; Exodus 19:5–6).

God made his will clear to the Israelites, and their disobedience was rightly referred to as being, "stiff-necked" and "hard-hearted." As Israel rebelled against God, they ignored the "goads" that God used to try to redirect them.

I wonder how the Lord looks at his church? Are we "Stiff Necked," unwilling to take direction and follow his lead? The apostle Paul tells us that there are carnal Christians that move and live in the flesh, (The Old Man of Sin)

To the Galatians, he said, *"O foolish Galatians, who hath bewitched you, that ye should not obey the truth, before whose eyes Jesus Christ hath been evidently set forth, crucified among you? This only would I learn of you, Received ye the Spirit by the works of the law, or by the hearing of faith? Are ye so foolish? having begun in the Spirit, are ye now made perfect by the flesh?"* Galatians 3:3

I think it is very important to explain the nature of carnality and show some examples. I say this because it raises its head in the lives of the Old Testament saints as well as those in the New Testament. It is that which fights against God and thwarts the progress of God's "Divine Destiny"

Here's the story about carnality and carnal Christians. It is offered by Dr. Michael Williams in an article published by the Christian Carrier, April 2015 edition.

Some of the best examples of why someone should be a Christian can be found in how some Christians live their lives. Likewise, some of the worst examples of why someone should be a Christian can be found in how some Christians live their lives.

By these two truths, many attitudes about Christianity are formed, unfortunately, often with deadly consequences. The Bible refers to Christians who are a poor example of Christianity as carnal. Therefore, we will examine what does it mean to be a carnal Christian?

**What does the word carnal mean?**

The word carnal is commonly defined as follows (1): carnal (adj): relating to physical, especially sexual needs and activities. "carnal desire" Origin: late Middle English: from Christian Latin carnalis, from caro, carn- 'flesh.'

The Bible defines the word carnal as follows (2): from G4561 (sarx); *pertaining to flesh*, i.e. (by extension) *bodily, temporal,* or (by implication) *animal, unregenerate*:- carnal, fleshly.

By these two definitions, we find that the word carnal describes something that is fleshly or physical in nature. The Bible adds to this the idea of being temporal, meaning that is earthly and temporary and not heavenly or eternal.

## What is a carnal Christian?

A "Carnal Christian" would be a Christian that behaves in ways that are motivated by fleshly desires. These desires are descried by the Bible as being human in origin, not from God, and demonstrated through human lusts. These three are *lust of the flesh, lust of the eyes, and pride of life* (1 John 2:15-16).

These lusts are what draw us away from God and tempt us to sin. Likewise, these lusts are what Satan uses to entice us to sin. We see the first use of these lusts in the Garden of Eden. Genesis 3:1-6).

In this passage, Satan enticed Eve by telling her that what God said about eating from the Tree of Knowledge of Good and Evil was not true. When her mind was changed, she wanted the fruit for three reasons.

1. She saw the fruit was good for food because of her hunger *(lust of the flesh)*.
2. See saw that it was pleasant to the eyes in appearance *(lust of the eyes)*.
3. And she desired it to make her wise like God *(pride of life)*.

Unfortunately, she listened to Satan, ate the fruit along with her husband, and sin entered mankind.

Likewise, fast forward several thousand years and we see the same approach used by Satan with Jesus in Luke 4:1-13. In this passage,

1. Satan tried to entice Jesus by telling him that if he was the Son of God to turn a stone into bread because of his hunger from fasting 40 days *(lust of the flesh)*.
2. Satan then tried to entice Jesus by taking him on a high mountain and telling him that if he bowed down and worshiped Satan, he could have everything he saw *(lust of the eyes)*.

3. Finally, Satan placed Jesus on top of the temple and tried to entice him by telling him that if he was the Son of God to throw himself off the temple because it is written that the angels would catch him (*pride of life*).

We learn from these events that unlike Eve, Jesus used Scripture every time Satan tried to entice him, even when Satan used Scripture out of context. This is where the carnal Christians stumble and fall. They do not know what the Bible says, or they flat-out ignore it when it comes to fleshly lusts. This demonstrates no love for God or for our neighbor.

**What are Biblical examples of carnal Christians?**

The most notable passage is when Paul addressed the church in Corinth as follows:

"And I, brethren, could not speak unto you as unto spiritual, but as unto carnal, *even* as unto babes in Christ. I have fed you with milk, and not with meat: for hitherto ye were not able *to bear it*, neither yet now are ye able. For ye are yet carnal: for whereas *there is* among you envying, and strife, and divisions, are ye not carnal, and walk as men? For while one saith, I am of Paul; and another, I *am* of Apollos; are ye not carnal? Who then is Paul, and who *is* Apollos, but ministers by whom ye believed, even as the Lord gave to every man?" (1 Corinthians 3:1-5)

In this passage, Paul had just spoken about how unsaved people could not understand the Bible, nor make sound decisions because they did not have the wisdom of the Holy Spirit (1 Corinthians 2). Paul called the unsaved man the natural man. Paul continued in 1 Corinthians 3 by saying that he could not speak spiritual things to these Christians because they were carnal in their thinking.

Paul went on to describe how he had trained them in the basic things, but that they had not grown in their faith so they could only handle the "milk" of the Word and not the "meat" of the Word. When Paul used these words, he was making a comparison between a baby and an adult. These Christians were still babies and not yet weaned off the simple teachings of Scripture (1 Corinthians 3:1-2).

The immaturity of these Christians resulted in behaviors that were based on fleshly, or carnal, motivations. They were envying one another, fighting, and the church was divided. He went on to describe how they had splintered into what we would call denominations today. The result of this carnal Christianity was that they were behaving like non-believers (1 Corinthians 3:3).

Being carnal was not limited to the church in Corinth. Even the Apostle Paul struggled at times with it (Romans 7:7-25). He described how it was a constant struggle to fight against the fleshly motivations within himself. The things he knew he should not do, he did and the things he knew he should do, he didn't do.

**What does God say about being carnal?**

The Bible tells us that the carnal mind is an enemy of God (Romans 8:7). It is the same thinking that non-believers have and is a result of the fall of man into sin (Genesis 3:15). God tells us that the remedy for being a carnal Christian is to remember that Christ died for us and will resurrect us. Because of this, we should seek to live for him because he loved us first (1 John 4:19) and we owe our salvation to him (Romans 8:10-17).

Finally, being carnal, not only shows we do not appreciate that Christ died for us, it shows non-Christians that being a Christian is no different from anyone else. This usually results in non-believers looking at Christians as hypocrites.

Worse yet, they see Christ as nothing special or different than any other religious figure. Sadly, this thinking, seals their demise and should break the hearts of every person who calls themself a Christian.

Being carnal demonstrates that we do not love God or our neighbor and leads others to believe that being a believer and follower of Christ is worthless. (Article by Dr. Michael L. Williams)

This carnality started with Adam & Eve and continues to this day.

How many Christians do you know that walk in the flesh and fit the profile of what the apostle John said? I would venture to say that in our modern times the number of carnal Christians exceeds 90%. That's just my personal observation. Maybe I do not walk in the right circles to see clearly. I see no real difference in the lost and the saved. More and more Christians act like unbelievers. They are out for themselves. Their greed and lust for power drives them. However, I could be wrong. What do you think?

We need to get our thinking in line with God' thinking. Here's how that can happen. Paul tells us, "*This I say then, walk in the Spirit and ye shall not fulfil the lust of the flesh. For the flesh lusts against the Spirit, and the Spirit against the flesh: and these are contrary the one to the other: so that ye cannot do the things that ye would.*" Galatians 5:16-17

I am so thankful that God has not given up on me. Even though I am fighting the natural man with all his evil, my Lord understands and shares his grace (Unmerited favor) with me to help me make it through this crazy upside-down world.

# CHAPTER THREE

## The Face of Divine Destiny In The Power of Good and Evil

We all should know that the power of good and the power of evil battle each other in the souls of men. Hear what the Bible says:

"*Do not be overcome by evil, but overcome evil with good.*" II Corinthians 6:14

This verse follows exhortations such as "Bless those who persecute you" (verse 14) and "Do not repay anyone evil for evil" (verse 17). The theme of the passage is how to love with sincerity (verse 9), and the instructions require us to set aside our natural inclinations.

God's way always challenges our fleshly nature and calls us to live at a higher level by the Spirit's power. The human way is to curse those who curse us and try to overcome evil with evil. But, according to Romans 12:21, we can only overcome evil with good. God's goodness is stronger than any evil. (Gotqueestions.com)

"*Woe unto them that call evil good, and good evil; that put darkness for light, and light for darkness; that put bitter for sweet, and sweet for bitter!*" Isaiah 5:20

Our divine destiny is to be like Jesus who indeed overcame evil with good. But, how does that actually happen? Come, let's reason together.

1. "Pray for them that despitefully use you." Romans 12:20
2. "If your enemy is hungry, give him food to eat; And if he is thirsty,

give him water to drink; For *so* you will heap coals of fire on his head, And the LORD will reward you." Proverbs 25:21-22

3. "Thou shalt love the Lord thy God with all thy heart, and with all thy soul, and with all thy mind. This is the first and great commandment. And the second is like unto it, *thou shalt love thy neighbor as thyself.*" Matthew 22: 36-39

4. "Therefore, all things whatsoever ye would that men should do to you, do ye even so to them; for this is the Law and the Prophets." Matthew 7:12

These are just a few ways: Love your neighbor, do not hold a grudge or use evil to fight back, focus on the Lord and his love which will give you power to overcome. It means we are not to hate, avenge, or mistreat others. Our mission is to operate in an attitude of love. Not easy to do, huh?

Our perspectives need to be thought out and examined for any falsehoods or erroneous conclusions. Many have built their perspectives on half-truths and downright error.

Recently, I discovered such a situation. There are those in the Christian community that tell us that we are in a continual battle with evil forces and we better have a clear perspective on the subject so we do not fall on the battlefield. I wholeheartedly agree with that view point but I do feel it needs a lot more discussion.

The issue is…do we live under the sovereignty of God, as his children, not really needing to fight the good fight of faith? Or…do we live in a world of sin and rebellion against God that requires us to be on guard all the time to protect ourselves and our families from Satanic attacks? Or…could it be a mix of both blended into a perspective that keeps us in God's eternal blessings?

Divine destiny comes from the sovereignty of God. The Sovereignty theory goes like this: Let's review.

If we rely completely on the sovereignty of God, we can rest in his divine care. The war between good and evil is over. God won. Lucifer, the devil or Satan, whoever we want to call him, was cast out of heaven with all his followers. They are now disembodied spirits placed is chains of darkness. *Jude 1:6*

They will never see the light of God's glory again until their final judgment. Therefore, there is no reason to worry. God is for us and has made provisions for us to be with him. He works all things together for good. *Spiritual warfare is no longer needed.* The battle is done, won, kaput. We are to live out our lives under God's grace. Wait a minute. Let's think about that.

If the war is over and Jesus really did totally defeat Satan, which he did:

Why does Paul tell us that fiery darts are being tossed at us? *Ephesians 6:16*

1. And why do we need to cast down every imagination and high thought that rises up above the knowledge of God? *II Corinthians 10:4-9*
2. If Satan has no weapons, why is he, as a roaring lion, attacking Christians? *I Peter 5:8-9*
3. Why are we asked to put on the whole armor of God? *Ephesians 6:10-16*
4. Why does Paul tell the church that their weapons are not carnal but mighty to the pulling down of strong holds? *2 Corinthians 10:4-5*
5. Why does the Bible say that we wrestle against principalities, against powers, against the rulers of the darkness of this world, against spiritual wickedness in high places? *Ephesians 6:12*
6. Why does God say "The angel of the Lord encamps round about them that fear (Reverence) him, to delivers them"? *Psalm 34:7*

Here's what I think about all of this:

The battle is over and we won but the war continues. Satan was stripped of any and all power by the finished work of Christ on the cross. *Colossians 2:15*

But Satan still wages war against the saints. He has no authority or spiritual weapons. He fights with lies, deception and snares, in hopes that he can trick the child of God into doing what he wants, thereby stealing his birthright, i. e. authority, power and dominion. John 10:10 It's all about deception and lies.

His lies have led many an unsuspecting soul down the road to destruction. Did you hear about the teenager that took drugs, just one time, and overdosed? In the hospital, the teen kept saying, "My friends said it was ok and I would feel great."

How about the girl that was told by her health clinic that her pregnancy was just a blob and she could abort it if she didn't want it? She didn't know that a fetus has a heartbeat within 5 ½ to 6-weeks of pregnancy. That's just about the time a girl would notice she is late. (By the way, California just passed a law that allows a girl to abort a baby up to 28-days AFTER it is born.) Go Figure!

Then there is the guy that realized he could enslave children and sell them to rich buyers, making lots of money.

These are just a few situations that actually happened because certain folks believed a lie and acted on it. They did the bidding of Satan whose goal is to kill, steal and destroy. Satan had no weapons or even an organized army. He uses deception and lies to get human beings to do what he wants.

**The Devil's Crowd**

It is true that our battle is with demons who are spiritual beings bent on our destruction. However, the devil also works through people. I call them, "The Devil's Crowd"

This group consists of folks that deny Jesus as coming in the flesh. They are those that the Bible calls, "anti-Christs." They are "False Prophets" and "False Teachers." They support abortion, same sex marriage, child pornography, wife swapping, human trafficking and the rest of the liberal agenda currently being pushed in our society. They are also in our churches distorting the truth and twisting the words of the Lord to meet their own needs.

Sadly enough, these folks could even be our parents, kids, neighbors, political officials, teachers and co-workers. Satan will use anyone to spread his "anti-Christ" message.

My wife, just for the fun of it, searched the Internet for crime in our area. She found all sorts of evil going on, all within one mile from our home. Now that's scary. However, as I said, Satan will use anyone that is not on guard spiritually to attack God's children. He has a host of demons that do his bidding and they are relentless. However, Jesus defeated all the powers of darkness and gave us his victory. In his name, we can overcome the wiles of the devil. We can overcome evil with good.

Satan's army is now the masses of the humanity. The Bible says, *"And every spirit that confesses not that Jesus Christ is come in the flesh is not of God: and this is that spirit of antichrist, whereof ye have heard that it should come; and even now already is it in the world."* I John 4:3

The battle these days is in the mind. We fight off the evil desires of our own hearts as well as the lies and suggestions of spirits that seek our harm. We also face the attitudes and criticism of that spirit of Anti-Christ who now operates in the children of disobedience.

It is important that we realize that God is sovereign and he is leading us through this upside-down crazy world. It is also important to see that we are in a life and death struggle with evil. Spiritual warfare is not dead. It is very alive and well. However, we are not asked to fight. Instead, we are asked to stand, wearing the armor of God and resist. The good fight of faith is to resist, holding fast the profession we declared when we were, "Born Again."

"If God be for us, who can be against us?" Romans 8:31 I can see lots of folks, lots of "Who" people that can and are against us. Here's what the Scripture says in Romans 8:30-34

"And those whom he predestined he also called, and those whom he called he also justified, and those whom he justified he also glorified. What then shall we say to these things? *If God is for us, who can be against us?*

He who did not spare his own Son but gave him up for us all, how will he not also with him graciously give us all things? Who shall bring any charge against God's elect? It is God who justifies. Who is to condemn?

Christ Jesus is the one who died—more than that, who was raised—who is at the right hand of God, who indeed is interceding for us."

It is true that we are the righteousness of God in Christ Jesus and therefore blameless in his sight. Here's how it looks in the scriptures:

- Even the righteousness of God *which is* by the faith of Jesus Christ unto all and upon all them that believe: Romans 3:22
- For therein is the righteousness of God revealed from faith to faith: as it is written, the just shall live by faith. Romans 1:17
- For he hath made him *to be* sin for us, who knew no sin; that we might be made the righteousness of God in him. 2 Corinthians 5:21

However, that does not exempt us from suffering persecution and demonic attacks. Remember what Jesus said to his disciples? *"Remember the word that I said unto you, the servant is not greater than his lord. If they have persecuted me, they will also persecute you; if they have kept my saying, they will keep yours also."* John 105:20

Who is it then that will come against the children of God? Is it not those that hate Jesus and do not believe in or obey him? The Bible calls these folks anti-Christ. As I said before, they do not believe that the Son of God came in the flesh and is the coming "Christ."

Paul did say that these anti-Christ have already invaded planet earth and dwell among us. They are actively warring against the saints to stop the spread of Christianity and discredit the message of the gospel.

I hold fast to what I have been saying all along. Jesus defeated the powers of darkness and gave us authority over them all so we, in his name, can not only stand against evil trickery, lies and snares but to actually take back what the devil has stolen.

We may not have the ability to rule over the entire earth but we, because of Jesus, can take dominion over our lives and situations that come our way. We can stand against the roaring lion of I Peter 5:8 resisting him in the faith and watch as he flees away in utter defeat.

We can hold up our "Shield of Faith" and see the fiery darts of hell being quenched.

We can, as 2 Corinthians 10:4-9 says, "cast down imaginations and every evil thought by bringing them into captivity to the obedience of Christ."

"Nay, in all these things we are more than conquerors through him that loved us." Romans 8:37 We are the children of God whose names are written in the Lamb's Book of Life and joint-heirs with Christ to a glorious destiny. This is the "Divine Perspective." This is the face of God's "Divine Destiny."

I am sure you have heard the saying, "Bad things happen when good folks do nothing." We cannot sit back and expect life to get better. There are those out there that seek to rule under an immoral, liberal view point that does not accept Christianity or the premise of morality, justice and fair play.

Our "Divine Destiny" is to take dominion over all that God brings into our life and rule over it with dignity and love. Kavish?

**Author's Note:** We have looked so far at God working out his divine will around the foolishness of sinful man. He has taken a back seat to our free will choices. However, this is just one side of the coin. The other side comes with a special relationship with the Lord that brings God close at hand.

Here are a few scriptures that support a close relationship with our Lord, just in case you don't agree.

"But God commended his love toward us, in that, while we were yet sinners, Christ died for us." Romans 5:8

"For God so loved the world, that he gave his only begotten Son, that whosoever believeth in him should not perish, but have everlasting life." John 3:16

"Behold, I stand at the door, and knock: if any man hear my voice, and open the door, I will come in to him, and will sup, (Dine),with him, and he with me." Revelation 3:20

"For I know the thoughts that I think toward you, saith the LORD, thoughts of peace, and not of evil, to give you an expected end." Jeramiah 29:11

"If we confess our sins, he is faithful and just to forgive us our sins, and to cleanse us from all unrighteousness." I John 1:9

"Behold, what manner of love the Father hath bestowed upon us, that we should be called the sons of God: therefore, the world knows us not, because it knew him not." I John 3:10

"The LORD thy God in the midst of thee is mighty; he will save, he will rejoice over thee with joy; he will rest in his love, he will joy over thee with singing." Zephaniah 3:17

"Jesus answered and said unto him, If a man love me, he will keep my words: and my Father will love him, and we will come unto him, and make our abode with him." John 14:23

"For ye have not received the spirit of bondage again to fear; but ye have received the Spirit of adoption, whereby we cry, Abba, Father." Romans 8:15

"The Spirit itself bears witness with our spirit, that we are the children of God:" Romans 8:16

"And if children, then heirs; heirs of God, and joint-heirs with Christ; if so be that we suffer with him, that we may be also glorified together." Romans 8:17

"Cast thy burden upon the LORD, and he shall sustain thee: he shall never suffer the righteous to be moved." Psalms 55:22

"Teaching them to observe all things whatsoever I have commanded you: and, lo, *I am with you always, even unto the end of the world.* Amen." Matthew 28:28

"Let us therefore come boldly unto the throne of grace, that we may obtain mercy, and find grace to help in time of need." Hebrews 4:16

"Casting all your care upon him; for he cares for you." I Peter 5:7

"For God hath not given us the spirit of fear; but of power, and of love, and of a sound mind" 2 Timothy 1:17

"Ask, and it shall be given you; seek, and ye shall find; knock, and it shall be opened unto you." Matthew 7:7

I think the above scriptures clearly indicate that God is for us and not against us. His love overshadows all of life and his will is available for the knowing and applying at a minute's notice.

It's great to hang out with your Heavenly Father and fellowship with Jesus through the Holy Spirit. This is why we were created, why we are here and is indeed the face of our "Divine Destiny." Prayers are answered, blessings are bestowed, love is given and accepted. What a life.

# CHAPTER FOUR

## The Face of Divine Destiny In The Restoration of a Nation

In chapter two, we saw Joseph's brothers sell him into slavery via a caravan to Egypt. During those days, Joseph went through a lot of things, too many to mention here. However, he ended up being next to the Pharoah in authority.

A famine caused his brothers to come to Egypt in search of grain, they discovered their heritage and a long story short, the entire family abandoned the promise land to dwell with Joseph in Egypt.

Years later, a new Pharoah came to power and put all of Abraham's family in bondage as slaves. They lived there in that way for over 400-years. The face of divine destiny drifted away into an alternate reality…until God raised up Moses to deliver his chosen people. Why so long in bondage? Here's what I see:

- The brothers had no regard for the life of their younger brother, Joseph.
- They did not consider the father's feelings towards Joseph and how he would be devastated.
- They obviously had little or no regard for the promise of Abraham's inheritance of the land and the making of a nation. They abandoned it for Egypt.

- They displayed the, "Stiff Necked" attitude, not willing to follow the promise of God to Abraham and the father's wishes.

Could it be that they wanted to live out their lives as they saw fit, not as God destined them? If that is the case, here's a scripture that fits them to a tee.

"Thou shalt not bow down thyself unto them, (False Gods) nor serve them; for I, the Lord thy God, am a jealous God, visiting the iniquity of the fathers upon the children unto the third and fourth generation of them that hate me," Deuteronomy 5:9

Joseph's brothers must have set themselves up as their own gods. It seems to me that they didn't care about anyone but themselves. Nevertheless, Abraham was informed by God about the bondage long before it happened. Take a read:

"Know for certain that your offspring will be sojourners in a land that is not theirs and will be servants there, and they will be afflicted for four hundred years." Genesis 15:13

God knows everything that will happen, and he revealed part of the future to Abraham. God's divine destiny was not bondage by decree from God. This scripture only tells us that God knew ahead of time and revealed it to Abraham.

We do not know for sure why the Jews spent 400+ years in bondage. I figure it was because of the wickedness of the brothers and how they treated Joseph. I figure it was also because their relationship with God as his children was in name only but they did what they wanted, seeking their own destiny.

In any event, the face of divine destiny now dwells in an alternate reality where God's children suffer and cry out for help that is not there for them. They did, however, learn humility, and were able to be molded by God into a solid nation, one in bondage, but still alive and hopeful for God's deliverance. God is at work, behind the scenes, working everything together for good.

Moses, an Old Testament foreshadow of Christ, is coming. He will rise to a position of power and lead God's people to freedom. God did not forget Israel and he will not forget us when we drift into an alternate reality.

How do you free a nation of slaves? Simple, toss out 10 or so really bad plagues upon the captors, kill their 1st born, and take all their gold and silver with you when you leave. It is estimated that 2 ½ million left Egypt to enter the wilderness so they could worship a God they knew little about and had never seen.

The miracles helped them to believe and trust the words of Moses. The opening of the Red Sea was a great visual demonstration of the power and authority of their unseen God. They were finally on their way to complete the promise God gave to Abraham.

God was working everything together for their good until the people started to long for the flesh pots of Egypt and got tired of the manna that fell from heaven every day. They lost interest in their unseen God and made a golden calf to worship.

If that wasn't bad enough, when they spied out the promised land, 10 of the 12 spies said the people were way greater than them and they were afraid to take the land. Their unbelief, after passing through the Red Sea and seeing all the plagues, caused God to once again let them wander, this time for 40 years in the desert. Some say the trip to their new home was somewhere from 3-11 days. Now, it will take 40 years and everyone over 20 will die in the wilderness.

Another alternate reality that didn't have to be. But it happened because of unbelief. How many alternate realities have you and I fallen into because we could not or would not believe God? Listen to what the Bible says:

"Harden not your hearts, as in the provocation, in the day of temptation in the wilderness: When your fathers tempted me, proved me, and saw my works forty years. Wherefore I was grieved with that generation, and said, They do always err in their heart and they have not known my ways.

So, I swear in my wrath, they shall not enter into my rest. *Take heed, brethren, lest there be in any of you an evil heart of unbelief, in departing from the living God.* But exhort one another daily, while it is called Today; lest any of you be hardened through the deceitfulness of sin. For we are made partakers of Christ, if we hold the beginning of our confidence steadfast unto the end;

While it is said, "Today if ye will hear his voice, harden not your hearts, as in the provocation."

For some, when they had heard, did provoke: howbeit not all that came out of Egypt by Moses. But with whom was he grieved forty years? Was it not with them that had sinned, whose carcasses fell in the wilderness? And to whom swear he that they should not enter into his rest, but to them that believed not? So we see that they could not enter in because of unbelief." Hebrews 3:8-19

# REST MY CHILD

Rest my child, says the Lord.
Take thy peace and be restored.
I have provided, thy mouth to feed.
From the beginning, I knew your need.
Do not worry, fret or even fear,
For, my child, I am always near
To bless thy soul with love and grace,
To be with thee, face to face.
Come, my child, near to my throne.
Do not allow your faith to roam.
For those who will not believe
Can never find rest in times of need.
My Word shall see you through.
My grace I freely give to you
That you should rest, thy soul to keep,
Forever delivered from unbelief.

Resting in the Lord is the best way to stay happy. However, it requires faith and trust in God that he will be there for you when you need him. It's kind of neat to relax when fear and anxiety are knocking at your door. Refusing to believe has its own path that leads to calamity and puts you outside of God's continual loving care.

So, the face of, "Divine Destiny" is hindered once again, being replaced with an alternative world for 40 years. But God does not abandon Israel, even though Israel abandoned him. He picks up with the next generation and leads them into the promise made long ago to Abraham. God's divine plan, the face of divine destiny, takes hold and becomes alive in his people.

God's sovereignty wins out, without damaging man's ability to freely choose his own destiny. The thing is, those that rebelled or scoffed at God's divine destiny die in the wilderness. All who do not want what God wants for them fall by the wayside. It goes to show you that it has always been God's way. Alternative realities just don't last. God wins. It's his way or the highway. But the highway leads to destruction.

The nation is in place and settled in the land. However, the battle for existence still goes on through the centuries. The Israelites drew close to God and were blessed and drifted away and suffered the horror of another reality under the oppression of other countries, all because they turned away from God to follow other gods or their own way.

From the Babylonian captivity to Hitler's attempt to exterminate the Jews in Nazi Germany, the face of divine destiny fell away and reappeared as the children of God fell away or drew near to God.

This is also a picture of the church. God's blessing and /or judgment waits for our free will decisions. Restoration has been promised and assured but the face of divine destiny has yet to bring forth its final results.

With reference to the nation of Israel, the Bible says:

- **Isaiah 11:12** – "And he shall set up an ensign for the nations, and shall assemble the outcasts of Israel, and gather together the dispersed of Judah from the four corners of the earth."
- **Ezekiel 37:12** – "Therefore prophesy and say unto them, Thus saith the Lord GOD; Behold, O my people, I will open your graves, and cause you to come up out of your graves, and bring you into the land of Israel."
- **Deuteronomy 30:3** – "That then the LORD thy God will turn thy captivity, and have compassion upon thee, and will return and gather thee from all the nations, whither the LORD thy God hath scattered thee."
- **Isaiah 66:8** – "Who hath heard such a thing? Who hath seen such things? Shall the earth be made to bring forth in one day? Or shall

a nation be born at once? For as soon as Zion travailed, she brought forth her children."

May 14, 1948 –A nation was born in a day. It all happened when the Jews declared independence for Israel as a united and sovereign nation for the first time in 2,900 years.

The church has followed the path of Israel over the centuries, drawing close and drifting away. However, it is even now being poised for the return of Jesus Christ. Every believer is being born in a day, the day they personally accept Christ as their savior. But the day is fast approaching when our Lord will gather us up together as a completed Holy Nation before God, the Father.

Peter tells us, *"But ye are a chosen generation, a royal priesthood, an holy nation, a peculiar people; that ye should shew forth the praises of him who hath called you out of darkness into his marvelous light; Which in time past were not a people, but are now the people of God: which had not obtained mercy, but now have obtained mercy."* I Peter 2: 9-10

This is the face of divine destiny that will culminate with the return of Jesus to planet earth and the gathering of his "Born Again" followers.

# CHAPTER FIVE

## The Face of Divine Destiny In A Crazy Upside-Down World

If your thinking is anything like mine, you will agree that we are living in the last days before Jesus returns and life on earth as we know it ends. Some of us may even live to see the Anti-Christ come to power. It will not be a fun time for those who are left behind when Jesus comes and goes.

Right now, we are living in those last days. I know that these are the last days because that which is good is called evil and evil good. Immorality is rampant in our society and folks are more and more becoming lovers of themselves and followers of pleasure, without regard for God or his will. This is a crazy upside-down world where every human life is at risk.

God wants us to fight the good fight of faith all the way to the end of the age. He wants us to stay free and live in good health and rule over our world until he comes back.

The end of the world is at hand but that does not mean we are to be slack or give up on what is true and right. Our job, as believers, is not to fall asleep at the wheel, but to stand and declare the goodness and love of God.

It is obvious that false prophets have come onto the world stage, as a "Pied Piper", and they have led many astray. It is also obvious that there has been, over the last 50 years, a great falling away from the faith and the doctrines taught by Jesus and his disciples.

I said all of that to say this. The same demons that led many to follow false prophets and believe in doctrines of devils in the 1st century are still here, hard at work, to take you down. We need to recognize what is happening around us. We need to discern the times we live in and we need to discover and apply the weapons of our warfare so we do not get lost in the crowd that is being led astray.

As I said in chapter three, the battle of the ages is for the souls of mankind. It all takes place in the mind of every human being. Before wars break out between countries, battles are fought and won or lost in the minds of the leaders of those nations. To survive in this crazy upside-down world, we will absolutely need to be able to recognize our enemy, know his dirty tricks and schemes, and what weapons God has provided for us to defend ourselves and even win the battle.

The face of divine destiny, that was hidden for the foundation of the world, is now known by his children. He has a master plan that is being worked out in the earth. All we need to do is trust him, believe his Word, apply his counsel and rest in his finished work of Grace.

I realize that times are worse than ever before, at least in our lifetime. There was a time when we didn't even have to lock our doors at night; when homosexuality was a sin before God; when sex before marriage was taboo; when a Politian tried to govern instead of following liberal agendas. What can we, as believers, do to get through this evil time? Here are some suggestions:

- **II Timothy 2:15**....*"Study to shew thyself approved unto God, a workman that needs not to be ashamed, rightly dividing the word of truth."*

The problem with today's Christians is most of them do not study the Bible to learn all there is. They do not know what God is saying to his children or the instructions he has left for them over the centuries. Thus, they cannot rightly divide the word of truth. We need to know in these last days.

- **II Corinthians 5:7**...*"walk by faith, not by sight"*

Our sight will most of the time deceive us because it is smeared over with false ads, false statements and false paths to follow. When we walk by faith, we walk in the scriptures, believing what is being said therein is for us and applicable to our life situations.

- **Hebrews 4:11**... *"labor therefore to enter into that rest, lest any man fall after the same example of unbelief."*

Resting in the power and authority of God is what it is all about. That is called, "Believing." That's what a believer does. If you need to labor or strive to attain that position, then do so immediately.

- **James 4:7**.... *"Submit yourselves therefore to God. Resist the devil, and he will flee from you."*

We cannot stand by idle while the devil destroys our life and happiness. Submission to the authority of God is essential and resisting is the key to success.

- **Proverbs 3:5-6**... *"Trust in the Lord with all thine heart; and lean not unto thine own understanding. In all thy ways acknowledge him, and he shall direct thy paths."*

We cannot lean to our own understanding of life and reality because our natural self is full of sin. Our perspective is greed, selfishness, lust and all the other deeds of the flesh as recorded in Galatians 5. When we acknowledge his will and Lordship, he will direct us. Try it and let me know how it goes.

- **I Thessalonians 5:18**... *"In everything give thanks: for this is the will of God in Christ Jesus concerning you."*

We are to give thanks to God *in every situation*. However, *not for every situation*. The giving of thanks is a way to let God know you are counting on him and believing that he will be there.

- **I John 2:15**... *"Love not the world, neither the things that are in the world. If any man loves the world, the love of the Father is not in him."*

The things of this world are centered in the pursuit of self-gratification. They do not emulate the love of God. If we get all caught up in the love of this world with all its lust, we will forfeit the love of God. We either want the love of God in us or the love of self. God is more important, don't you think?

- **Galatians 5:16**…"*Walk in the Spirit, and you shall not fulfill the lust of the flesh.*"

Walking in the Spirit brings fellowship with God and frees you from the evil actions of the flesh. There is joy and happiness in God's Spirit. There is only sorrow and pain in fleshly living.

- **Proverbs 4:23**…"*Keep thy heart with all diligence: for out of it are the issues of life*"

Keeping your heart is to guard it as though it was in danger of being stolen or spoiled. We are to watch over it because from it comes the issues of life.

- **Mark 12:30**…"*Love the Lord thy God with all thy heart, and with all thy soul, and with all thy mind, and with all thy strength*"

Loving God should be a continual thing and done with all our energy and heart. It is a romance, a love story and a blessing in every way.

- **Matthew 6:34**…"*Take therefore no thought for the morrow: for the morrow shall take thought for the things of itself. Sufficient unto the day is the evil thereof.*"

Worry is a sin. We are constantly instructed by the scriptures to "Fret Not" "Do not fear" and so on. Yes, evil is out there but our God is greater and he has surrounded us with his love. He will provide, deliver, keep and restore…not to worry.

- **2 Corinthians 6:14**…"*Be ye not unequally yoked together with unbelievers: for what fellowship hath righteousness with unrighteousness? and what communion hath light with darkness?*"

Unequally yoked is hanging around with unbelievers more than with the children of God. Who you hang out with will determine the course of actions you follow in life. What is it about the birds of a feather? Oh yea, they flock together.

- Colossians 3:15…"*Let (Allow) the peace of God to rule (Referee) in your heart.*"

If you let or allow the peace of God to be the referee in your thought life and daily actions, you will assuredly stay on the right path. No peace? Take No action!

- **Romans 12:21**…"*Be not overcome of evil, but overcome evil with good.*"

Never use evil to avenge evil. That action just pulls you down to the level of the evil doer and it robs God of the right to repay or judge the offense. Instead, try doing good to overcome evil. That is God's way of doing things.

- **Matthew 7:7** …"*Ask, and it shall be given you; seek, and ye shall find; knock, and it shall be opened unto you.*"

Ask, Seek and Find. This is the formula for good communication with God. Use it liberally during your journey towards eternity. It will serve you well.

- **Romans 12:20**…"*Pray for them that despitefully use you.*"

Praying is always a good thing. When you pray for those that hate you, it keeps you from being attached to that person by hate. It also takes away the torment of rehashing the matter over and over in your mind.

- **Matthew 22: 36-39**… "*love thy neighbor as thyself.*"

If we love our neighbor as ourselves, we eliminate prejudice, hate, division, race inequality and a whole lot more that is even now destroying our society.

- **Matthew 7:12**…"*Therefore, all things whatsoever ye would that men should do to you, do ye even so to them; for this is the Law and the Prophets.*"

It is a good thing to treat other folks as you would want them to treat you. That means with love and dignity, respect and honor. That's a good "Rule of Thumb."

- **Ephesians 6:10-16**…"*Put on the whole armor of God.*"

Wearing the whole armor of God is essential in being safe, especially in an upside-down world like we live in. The suit of armor is really cool. You get a helmet of salvation, a breastplate of righteousness, shoes that are made with the gospel of peace, a loin belt made from truth and even the sword of the spirit to quench fiery darts.

- **Philippians 4:8**… *"Finally, brethren, whatsoever things are true, whatsoever things are honest, whatsoever things are just, whatsoever things are pure, whatsoever things are lovely, whatsoever things are of good report; if there be any virtue, and if there be any praise, think on these things."*

We think a lot these days about a lot of stuff. Some of our thoughts tend to be negative and depressing. After all, we live in a crazy world with rising crime, abortion, political unrest etc. The best remedy is to shift your thinking to good things and focus on happy not sad. Remember, as a man or woman thinks in the heart, so is he/she. Proverbs 23:7

You can probably find more scriptures that direct you on how to live and what to do in these last days. The thing is, God wants you to participate in shaping the face of his divine destiny. Live in these scriptures and you will be ok. Do what they say to do and you will be taking dominion of your life situations.

He does not want you to do your own thing because that course of action leads down the road to destruction. We need to be pliable in the hands of our creator so he can prepare us for his kingdom and shape us into his immage.

The interesting thing, as I see it, is that it's all about God and yet he includes us in that destiny. We are to live, move and have our being in him. Why? because we are his offspring. Acts 17:28

The promise of Romans 8:28-30 is a strong force in taking us through a crazy upside-down world. God is with us and he is actively working all things together for our good. We love God and are called according to his purposes and he loves us. What more could we ask for. What a destiny.

# CONCLUSION

The face of divine destiny is a Godly perspective that ensures his will is accomplished in the earth and for all eternity. It is the accomplishment of his sovereignty.

I hope I have shown a clear picture of God's divine destiny. His will and objectives are the only things that counts. Our will is always subject to sin and cannot sustain a happy lifestyle. We need God and we need to know his will to have life. He knows the future. He knows the difficulties and challenges we face and will face. He has promised that he will be with us always and guide us, counsel us and even protect us.

We must, above all else, relinquish our hold on our will and submit to his will. He must lead and we must follow. Doing this simple thing will help us avoid alternate realities and keep us on track for continual blessings.

Let us follow after him, denying ourselves and worshiping Jesus as Lord and Savor. Salvation is at hand. Grab it while you can.

# ABOUT THE AUTHOR
# JOHN MARINELLI

Rev. Marinelli is an ordained minister, He has formed and been pastor of one church in Wisconsin and was the pastor of another in Alabama. He has also been a youth minister and evangelism director over the years.

Rev. Marinelli has authored several other books including: "Original Story Poems", "The Art of Writing Christian Poetry," "Pulpit Poems," "Moonlight & Mistletoe," "The Mysterious Stranger," "With Eagles Wings," "Mysteries & Miracles," "It Came To Pass," Why Do The Righteous Suffer," "Believer's Handbook of battle Strategies." "Hidden In Plain Sight" "The End of The World, From The Beginning, Shadows in the Light of a Pale Moon," "Mister Tugboat" "An Elephant Named Clyde" "Morning Reign" "Times Past But Not Forgotten" "How To Be Happy" and "How To Have A Victorious Christian Life."(www.marinellichristianbooks.com)

John is an accomplished Christian poet. He also dabbles in songwriting, likes to play chess, sings karaoke and goes fishing now and then. He lives in north central Florida where he enjoys a retired lifestyle with his wife and two collies.

# GALLERY OF ENCOURAGING CHRISTIAN POEMS

# AGREEING WITH GOD

We speak of things that are not,
Believing in them as though they were,
Because our Heavenly Father spoke them first,
Sending them to us in promises that never blur.

We take Him at His Word,
And listen to all He has to say.
We wrap each promise around our souls,
Until what was spoken becomes our day.

We will agree with the Lord,
Trusting that He knows best.
For only His awesome power,
Can provide our souls with rest.

"As it is written, I have made thee a father of many nations, before Him who he believed, even God who quickens the dead and calls those things that be not as though they were" Romans 4:17

Like Abraham, we also have a destiny that God has spoken into our lives. He calls it forth before it exists. Like Abraham, we are to believe, even against hope, that what God said will indeed come to be. (Romans 4:18).

# ARM'S LENGTH

I hold the world at arm's length,
That its choices do not interfere.
While it does its own thing,
I watch and wait over here.

My steps must not go that way,
For it's not where I need to be.
The Lord has shown me the path,
That will lead me to my destiny.

The call of the world is strong
And pulls at me now and then.
But I know that way
Is full of sorrow and sin.

I must move on in life
Beyond their beckoning call.
It's the right thing to do,
So I do not stumble or fall.

I will not be swayed or misled
By family, friends or business deal.
Their secret thoughts are not mine,
To consider, to admire or feel.

So I keep the world at "Arm's Length"
As I journey through this life.
My faith in Jesus keeps me strong,
As I walk in His glorious light.

"Love not the world, neither the things that are in the world. If any man loves the world, the love of the Father is not in him. For all that is in the world, the lust of the flesh, the lust of the eyes and the pride of life, is not of the Father, but of the world. And the world passes away and the lust thereof: But he that doeth the will of God abides forever. I John 2:15-17

It is more important to know God and to follow after Him, than to become entangled in life's lustful traps: for if we were to gain the whole world and lose our own soul, how terrible would that be?

# DON'T WORRY

Don't worry about tomorrow.
You did that yesterday.
Go on with your life
And remember always to pray.

Ask and it shall be given to you,
But this great truth you already know.
Rejoice and be happy, why? Because…
Your harvest comes from what you sow.

I will say it again and even more,
Until it becomes very very clear.
Tomorrow will take care of itself,
But worry is another word for fear.

Now here's what I want you to do.
Trust in the Lord and be of good cheer.
Drop the worry from your vocabulary
And cast out that demon of fear.

Worry is the flipside of faith. If you are walking in faith, you are free from worry. Why, because faith hopes in God and trusts that he will be there to meet your need.

# TWO HOUSES

We built our homes together,
Mine upon a Rock and his in the sand.
He thought his would be all right,
But he was a foolish man.

God's wisdom showed me the way.
And what I needed to do,
But my foolish neighbor,
Never had a clue.

Then the rains came,
And the winds began to blow.
The storms beat upon our homes,
And we had nowhere to go.

We built our homes together,
My neighbor and me.
Mine is still there upon the Rock,
But his ceased to be.

Wise men and fools both suffer,
The storms that befall mankind.
But those who trust in Jesus
Will always stand the test of time.

Foundation is everything. If you build your life on the Word of God, it will last forever. That's why we strive to be obedient to the will of God. We want his destine and his blessings, no matter what the world system thinks or does.

# CLUTTER

Clutter keeps the mind confused,
As images dance through the night.
Lost among those unimportant thoughts,
Are the dreams that once shined bright.

An endless parade of fear and doubt,
Crowds the mind to destroy our day.
Ever soaring on the wings of the soul,
Until it has formed an evil array.

But clutter is by one's choice,
Of those who dance to its beat.
Better to face imaginations' due
Than to fall into utter defeat.

Be Quiet!!! Is our spirit's desperate cry,
As we call upon the name of the Lord.
Silence is our heart's desired prayer,
Until our minds are again restored.

"Keep thy heart with all diligence: for out of it are the issues of life" Proverbs 4:23

We make the final choices in life that either lead us astray or closer to the Lord. We chose what enters our hearts and fills our minds. May we always choose the path of righteousness and the way of peace.

# THE LORD'S LITTLE TWO BY FOUR

God has a little 2' X 4'
That rest on heaven's windowsill.
He uses it now and then,
When we stray from His will.

Sometimes we need a good "Bap";
With the Lord's little 2' X 4'
To knock out the confusion,
And help us to desire Him more.

The Lord's little 2' X 4'
Is what we sometimes need,
To get our thinking straight,
And keep our focus indeed.

The Lord's little 2' X 4'
Is fashioned from life's every trial,
So we do not stray from His will,
Or fall into an ungodly lifestyle.

"My son, despise not the chastening of the Lord; neither be weary of His correction: for whom the Lord loves, He corrects; even as a father his son, in whom he delights." Proverbs 3:11 & 12

It is a good thing to be corrected by God. We should not fear His rebuke for it is not His wrath, but rather a blessing from His love that keeps us moving on towards maturity.

# I FIND MYSELF IN GOD

I find myself in God.
He is my, "Everything"
I know that He is Lord,
My Life, My Hope, My King.

I find myself in God,
Not the ways of Sin.
Nor do I look to others,
To know who I really am.

I find myself in God,
To whom I bow on bended knee.
He alone is my joy and strength
And where I want to be.

"For we are His workmanship, created in Christ Jesus unto good works, which God hath before ordained, that we should walk in them" Ephesians 2:10

Knowing that we are created in Christ Jesus gives us confidence to walk in Christ, as He walked, along a pathway of good works. It is our joy and pleasure to be like Him. In Him we move and live and have our being.

# "I AM" THERE

**"I AM"** There,
At the end of your broken dreams,
Before the sun rises over your day,
Prior to those tear-filled streams.

**"I AM"** There,
Down that road of despair,
When all appears to be lost,
And no one seems to care.

**"I AM"** There,
Over all of life's twists and turns,
When tomorrow is all but gone,
And when you are full of concerns.

**"I AM"** There,
Sayeth the Lord of Host,
To bring you hope and peace,
And the power of My Holy Ghost.

**"I AM"** There,
To be sure you make it through,
In the midst of every trial,
To bless your life and deliver you.

**"I Am" There**

"All power is given unto me in heaven and earth. Go ye therefore and teach all nations, baptizing them in the name of the Father, and of the Son, and of the Holy Ghost: Teaching them to observe all things, whatsoever I have commanded you: and lo, I am with you always, even unto the end of the world." Mathew 28:18-20

The Lord is with us always. He never leaves our side, even when we leave His. In every situation, He is there. It's time to count on His presence and trust in His care.

# SO LISTEN UP

I write this verse that all should know.
What I have to say is like a seed, ready to grow.
So listen up to all I have to say.
It could be the very blessing your heart needs today.

God has not given you a spirit of fear.
Instead, He has offered to dry up every tear.
He really loves you, even though you often fail.
His love and mercy follows you,
Enabling you to be the head and not the tail.
So do not worry or even fret.
That's why Jesus paid sin's awful debt.
Now go on in life to discover its victory
Knowing that Jesus has indeed set you free.

"For God hath not given us the spirit of fear: but of Power and of Love and a sound mine" II Timothy 1:7

There is nothing to fear except fear itself and that spirit has been defeated on the cross. We now have the Spirit of power and love and a sound mind. He will never leave us or forsake us. We are truly free.

# WINNING THE BATTLE

We must use the Word of God
To calm emotions that fray.
For the enemy never sleeps,
Until he has led us astray.

So when your emotions overflow
With feelings like depression and fear.
Know this! If you dwell in that place,
You invite the enemy to draw near.

When your emotions rage
With fiery darts aglow,
Stand in the power of the Lord,
Against its awful woe.

And if you get confused
And lost in the storm,
Put your thoughts on trial,
Rejecting all but heaven born.

You can win the battle
That rages within your soul.
By casting down imaginations,
And breaking Satan's hold.

Remember to focus on Jesus,
Holding the world at arm's length.
Lift up your head above the trial,
And the Lord will give you strength.

"For the weapons of our warfare are not carnal but mighty, through God, to the pulling down of strongholds: casting down imaginations and every high thing that exalts itself against the knowledge of God, and bringing into captivity every thought to the obedience of Christ." II Corinthians 10:3-5 The battle is in our minds and we win by putting our thoughts on trial and casting out all that oppose the knowledge of God. This is true victory.

# THE LIGHTHOUSE

A lighthouse is a blessing,
To the ships that toss in the sea.
For it shows them the way,
Until they can clearly see.

The rage of an angry storm,
Cannot hide its brilliant light.
Nor can its awesome furry,
Rule as an endless night.

Jesus is the lighthouse,
For those who have gone astray.
The light of His love,
Offers a new and living way.
Jesus is the lighthouse,
When fear and sickness rage.
The light of His love,
Gives hope in difficult days.

So trust in the Lord,
And look for His light.
He alone is "The Lighthouse",
That guides you through the night.

"I am the Way, the Truth, and the Life. No man cometh to the Father but by me" John 14:6

Life holds many dark nights that are full of unexpected storms. Only a deep abiding faith in Jesus Christ will get us through. He is the light of the world. His light keeps us from falling into confusion, sorrow, sickness and demonic oppression.

# THE WAY MAKER

Only Jesus can make a way,
Through the difficulties of life.
He alone is Lord and King,
Over life's sorrows and strife.

He is the "Way Maker,"
When there is no visible way.
He will make the way known,
As though it were the light of day.

He will make a way,
For those of humble heart.
He will clear away the rubble,
Restoring what Satan broke apart.
Jesus is the "Way Maker,"
A friend to all who are lost.
He has made the way,
Paying sin's incredible cost.

The way to the Maker,
Is through His only Son.
He alone is the "Way Maker,"
Until life's battles are won.

"Let not your heart be troubled. Ye believe in God, believe also in me. In my father's house are many mansions: If it were not so, I would have told you. I go to prepare a place for you. And if I go and prepare a place for you, I will come again, and receive you unto myself, that where I am, there ye may be also." John 14: 1-3

The Lord is prepared for any emergency. He knows the beginning from the end and has gone before us to prepare a way that we can follow until we see Him face to face.

# STINKING THINKING

Stinking thinking, they say,
Is bad for your health.
For it frustrates life's goals,
And denies happiness and wealth.

A right perspective is important,
As we think about everything.
It will either bring us down,
Or cause us to shout and sing.

What we think about these days,
Really does affect our life.
It can cause us to overflow with Joy,
Or fall into depression and strife.

So don't let your thinking,
Stink all the way up to heaven.
Stand in faith before God,
And get rid of that negative leaven.

"Then Jesus said unto them, take heed and beware of the leaven of the Pharisees and the Sadducees" Mathew 16:6

Someone once said, "We are what we think" The Bible says, "As a man thinks, so is he" It is important to concentrate our thinking of those things that are of good report, pure, honest and that will keep us clean of heart.

# WISE MEN STILL SEEK HIM

Wise men still seek Him
Who appeared so long ago.
They come now by grace
Through faithful hearts aglow.

Wise men still seek Him
For He is their "Bread of Life."
A sustaining inner strength
Through times of sorrow or strife.

Wise men still seek Him
The Christ of Calvary.
God's only begotten Son
Crucified as Sin's penalty.

Wise men still seek Him
Jesus, God in human array.
King of kings & Lord of lords
Born to earth on Christmas Day.

"Now when Jesus was born in Bethlehem of Judea in the days of Herod the king, behold, there came wise men from the east to Jerusalem, saying, where is he that is born king of the Jews? For we have seen his star in the east and are come to worship him" Mathew 2:1-2

Seeking Jesus is the wisest thing any man, woman or child can do and when we find Him, it is our privilege to bow down and worship Him. This is our journey, our destiny and our life while on this earth.

# THE ANGELS CRY HOLY

The Angels cry "Holy,"
While sorrow fills the land.
For God's Judgment Day,
Is to come upon every man.

The Angels cry "Holy,"
While mankind goes astray,
Rejecting the love of God,
To follow his own precarious way.

The Angels cry "Holy,"
Knowing the terror of the Lord,
When all who dwell in sin,
Will suddenly be destroyed.

The Angels cry "Holy,"
Waiting for all things new,
Born of the Holy Spirit,
When God's Judgment is through.

The Angels cry "Holy,"
"Holy is the Lamb,"
Waiting for the children of God,
To join "The Great I AM"

"And one cried unto another and said, "Holy, Holy, Holy, is the Lord of host: the whole earth is full of his glory" Isaiah 6:3

We serve a Holy God that deserves our reverence and homage. The angels know this and worship Him, but man, because of sin, has no real concept of his own creator.

# A HIGHWAY CALLED "HOLINESS"

He places my feet on
A highway called "Holiness,"
That led my soul
To the throne of God.

Amidst the cheers of angels,
I walk, wearing His holy gown.
Onward towards heaven's throne,
While evil cast its awful frown.

My eyes were opened
That I might see.
Both the good and the evil,
That sought after me.

I walk the highway-Holiness
That crosses all of time.
Towards the throne of God,
Leaving this world behind.

"And an highway shall be there, and a way, and it shall be called, the way of holiness; the unclean shall not pass over it; but it shall be for those: the wayfaring men, though fools, shall not err therein. No lion shall be there, nor any ravenous beast shall go up thereon, it shall not be found there, but the redeemed shall walk there. And the redeemed of the Lord shall return, and come to Zion with songs and everlasting joy upon their heads: They shall obtain joy and gladness, and sorrow and sighing shall flee away. " Isaiah 35:8-10

What a privilege to walk the highway of Holiness. It is prepared especially for us, the redeemed, and it is protected from the errors of fools and the snarl of beast and especially the roar of the lion.

# CALL UPON THE LORD

When your burdens overwhelm you,
Like a mighty raging sea.
Call upon the Lord, Jesus,
And He will set you free

When your heartaches are many,
And life is difficult to understand.
Call upon the Lord, Jesus.
He will come and hold your hand.

When your friends reject you,
Because you follow after Him,
Call upon the Lord, Jesus.
And keep yourself from sin.

When you fall into depression,
As though it were a giant pit.
Call upon the Lord, Jesus,
Who will restore your joyful wit.

When you're saddened by the day
Feeling lost and all alone.
Call upon the Lord, Jesus,
Who will make His way known.

When you are weary and heavy laden,
Tired from life's many tests.
Call upon the Lord, Jesus,
Who is sure to give you rest.

"Hear my cry; oh God, attend unto my prayer. From the end of the earth,

I will cry unto thee, when my heart is overwhelmed: Lead me to the rock that is higher than I." Psalms 61:1-2

Calling upon the Lord in stressful times is o.k. He wants us to cry to Him and then to trust in Him to watch over His Word to perform it on our behalf.

# IT CAME TO PASS

Things often come to pass,
But seldom do they ever last.
They come into our busy day,
For awhile, then pass away.

We hear their voices, loud and clear,
As they arrive and while they are here.
They speak both joy and misery,
Some to you and some to me.

We say, "It came to pass,"
Or say, "It happened so fast."
Down life's beaten path,
Comes both love and wrath.

So say goodbye to sad and blue.
To all that is now troubling you.
For things will come, only to pass,
But God's love will always last.

"And it came to pass in those days…" Luke 2:1

These are the times of our lives. We live them, some for good and some for not so good. One thing is for sure, that which comes our way, comes only to pass on by. It is not what happens that is so important, but rather what we do with what we are faced with.

Trusting in the Lord and seeking His guidance will always conquer that which comes to pass.

# THE WHOSOEVER SCENARIO

The "Whosoever" is who so ever,
Not who so won't, can't or will not.
The story is as clear as a sunny day.
God offers a new and living way.

But only those who engage "free will"
To choose life, faith and obedience,
Will find salvation for their souls,
And be cleansed and made whole.

We do the choosing: to accept or deny.
That is how God set it up to be.
He made the call to life's "Whosoever",
That they could live abundantly.

"For God so loved the world, that he gave his only begotten son, that whosoever believeth in him, should not perish but have everlasting life." John 3:16

We are the "Whosoever" in John 3:16, that one day put his or her faith in Christ, believed in Him and now rest in the Lord's love and grace. We have the promise of God that He sent His Son so we could believe and have everlasting life. How great is that?

# LITTLE PRISONS

Little prisons await the man with a lustful soul.
Bars of selfishness and pride create dungeons of icy cold.

Prisons of shame and jealousy fill the heart with utter despair.
Bars that separate from God and those that really care.

Stand back! While the doors are tightly closed;
Taking away your life, to wither as a dying rose.

Beware of those little prisons that trap the lustful soul.
Keep yourself free from sin through faith in the Christ of old.

Little prisons need not to be your fate.
It is your choice, Spirit or flesh to date.

"O Foolish Galatians, who hath bewitched you, that ye should not obey the truth, before whose eyes Jesus Christ hath been, evidently set forth, crucified among you? Are you so foolish? Having begun in the Spirit, are you now made perfect in the flesh?

We should always seek to dwell in the Spirit, that we would not emulate the deeds of the flesh. When we fall short, we create "little prisons" that keep us in confusion and away from the blessing of God. It's time to walk in the Spirit and break the prisons that so easily beset us.

# A WHISPER IN THE WIND

There's a whisper in the wind
That lingers both day and night.
A champion of truth and justice,
By the power of His might.

A word in due season
That echoes from deep within.
A voice out of nowhere,
Reproving the world of sin.

Look there, in the street
And here, by the shores of the sea.
There's a whisper hidden in the wind;
A voice from eternity.

There's a calling from God.
His voice is hidden in the wind.
In a whisper, He speaks to our hearts
With the love and counsel of a friend.

Listen for the Whisper,
All who seek to know.
It is God's Holy Spirit
Telling you which way to go.

"And thine ears shall hear a word behind thee saying, This is the way, walk ye in it, when ye turn to the right hand and when ye turn to the left" Isaiah 30:21

The voice of the Lord is often a still small voice, yet always clear and it never brings confusion. His voice is like a whisper in the wind that brings a peaceful breeze to the heart. The joy of hearing His voice is to know His will and our destiny.

# FRAGILE FLOWER RED

As a flower in earthen sod,
I bloom for thee, oh God.
To blossom with the turn of spring;
To be to you, a beautiful thing.

I lift my Fragile Flower Red
Upward from my earthen bed;
To draw light from God above,
Strength and peace and joy and love.

As a flower, I bloom for thee
That passersby may stop and see.
Your fragrance and beauty I am,
Flowered in grace as a man.

As a flower in earthen sod,
I bloom for thee, oh God.
Upward, I lift my head,
As a Fragile Flower Red.

"Be not conformed to this world, but be ye transformed, by the renewing of your mind, that ye may prove what is that good and acceptable and perfect will of God."

When we look to God as our source, we blossom, much like a flower that draws light from the sun. When we blossom, like a flower, we display the glory and beauty of our creator to all who care to stop and look. This is our divine destiny.

**Other books by John Marinelli can be viewed and purchased at:** www.marinellichristianbooks.com

www.ingramcontent.com/pod-product-compliance
Lightning Source LLC
Chambersburg PA
CBHW020430010526
44118CB00010B/507